# PROJECT 17:17

My friend is
struggling with

# CONFLICTS

with others

D0189409

PROJECT 17:17

My friend is
struggling with

# CONFLICTS

with others

# Josh
McDowell
&
Ed Stewart

**CF4•K**

Conflicts with Others ISBN: 978-1-84550-354-3
© 2000 Josh McDowell and Ed Stewart
First published by Josh McDowell Ministries in 2000
www.josh.org
This edition published in 2008 by Christian Focus
Publications, Geanies House, Fearn, Tain, Ross-shire,
IV20 1TW, Great Britain. www.christianfocus.com

Cover design by Daniel van Straaten

Printed by Nørhaven Paperback A/S

Scripture quotations used in this book are from the
Holy Bible, New International Version. Copyright ©
1973, 1978, 1984, International Bible Society. Used by
permission of Zondervan Bible Publishers.

Themes:  Conflict management; Youth-conduct;
Interpersonal relations; Christian life.

We would like to thank the following people:

David Ferguson, director of Intimate Life Ministries of Austin, Texas, has made a tremendous contribution to this collection.

Dave Bellis, my (Josh) associate of twenty-three years, labored with us to mold and shape each book in this collection. Each fictional story in all eight books in the PROJECT 911 collection was derived from the dramatic audio segments of the "Youth in Crisis Resource," which Dave personally wrote. We are so very grateful for Dave's talents and involvement.

Joey Paul of Word Publishing not only believed in this entire project, but also consistently championed it throughout Word.

Titles in this series:

978-1-84550-354-3
My Friend is Struggling with Conflicts with Others


978-1-84550-355-0
My Friend is Struggling with the Death of a Loved One


978-1-84550-356-7
My Friend is Struggling with Finding True Love


978-1-84550-357-4
My Friend is Struggling with Thoughts of Suicide

Project Partners:

Christian Focus Publications
Geanies House
Fear, Tain, Ross-shire
IV20 1TW, Scotland, U.K.
www.christianfocus.com

Josh McDowell Ministry
P.O. Box 131000
Dallas, TX 75313-1000
U.S.A.

Agapé
Fairgate House, Kings Road
Tyseley, Birmingham B11 2AA
Telephone 0121 765 4404
www.agape.org.uk

# CONTENTS

# KEN'S STORY

**W**HEN HIS DAD WALKED INTO THE room, fifteen-year-old Ken Meyers knew what he would say. This conversation happened at least once a week during the school year, sometimes twice.

"I thought you had homework to do," Dad said, lifting the headphones from Ken's ears and placing them on the bedside table. Ken bristled inside. He felt like a little kid when his dad took things away from him like that.

Ken, who had been lying on his bed listening to music, sat up. "I do have homework," Ken said, displaying the language-arts worksheet in his hand, "and I'm doing it." He was about halfway through an exercise of diagramming sentences.

"You know you will concentrate better without that noise rattling your brain." Dad motioned toward the headphones, which were plugged into Ken's portable CD player. The music was still playing, but it was faint and tinny coming from the tiny headphone speakers on the table.

"It's not noise, Dad; it's music – Christian music," Ken said respectfully. He hated his dad's frequent lectures, but it only got worse if Ken let his attitude get the best of him.

Dad's hands went to his hips, his classic lecture pose. "That is not music, Kenneth. It sounds like a bunch of spoons caught in the garbage disposal. Just because a group says it is Christian doesn't mean its message is coming from God."

Ken wanted to argue the point.

*Listen to the words, Dad. They are just as biblical as any of those cassettes of hymns you and Mom play. As for the music, it's a "joyful sound." You're so paranoid that I might be listening to satanic music.*

But he had tried that approach before, and the lecture had only lasted longer. So Ken kept his thoughts to himself.

"Besides, I could never do homework with the TV or radio on," his dad continued. "It ruins your concentration."

*It may ruin your concentration, Dad, but it doesn't ruin mine. The music actually keeps me relaxed and helps me concentrate. Can't you accept that my study habits could be different from yours?*

Ken felt the anger steaming up inside him, but he kept silent.

"You can't afford to waste study time, Kenneth. Your grades are slipping. This is not middle school, son. You have to bear down if you want to achieve the grades that will get you into State University."

*I've tried to tell you that I don't want to go to State, Dad,* Ken argued silently. *In fact, I don't think I want to go to any college right after high school. I want to take at least one year off to travel with a Christian band or to take a short-term missions trip. Maybe then I'll know what I want to do with my life. If you would only listen to me sometime you might* understand what's going on in my life. But all you can think about are my grades.

"And what about these?" his dad pressed. The man's hand left his hip long enough to point to the shoebox on the bed next to Ken.

"Those are my baseball cards."

"I can see that they are baseball cards, Kenneth," his dad snapped. "I mean, what are they doing here beside you while you are studying?"

"I don't study every single minute, Dad," Ken snapped back. "I keep them here so I can look at them when I need a break."

"It's just another temptation to waste time," his dad said firmly. Then he reached out as if to take the box away.

Ken grabbed the box, ready to pull it back. "It's my hobby, Dad," he argued. "Don't worry, I'm not going to fail English because I look at a few cards now and then." Ken had allowed his sarcasm to come out a little too strongly, and he wished he could take it back.

For a moment Ken and his father eyed each other without speaking, each with a hand on the box of baseball cards. "I'm going to put these cards away so they won't distract you," Dad said, starting to pull from his end of the box.

Common sense told Ken to let go of the box and to drop the argument. But he was too mad to listen to his better judgment. "They're not distracting me, Dad. I can study just as well with-"

Ken's end of the box tore open in the subtle tug-of-war, and more than three hundred baseball cards spilled onto the bed and the floor. His dad was left holding the torn and suddenly empty shoebox. Ken wished he hadn't been so bull-headed, but he was tired of caving in when his parents tried to mold him into their idea of a student. He had never resisted his father like this before, and he was a little afraid of the possible consequences.

Dad studied the mess of cards for a moment then glared at his son. Ken was afraid that the baseball cards were history. Instead, Dad dropped the box to the floor and scooped up the CD player and carry-case of CDs from the bedside table. "I don't want to see these again, Kenneth," he announced, shaking his finger at the mess of cards, "and you won't be listening to this so-called music until your GPA comes up a full point." Then he left the room, closing the door behind him.

Ken was so angry he almost cried. If it wasn't his grades or music Dad and Mom disapproved of, it was his clothes or his hairstyle or his friends. His baseball-card collection was "frivolous," they said. (He should get into biking or rock climbing, something that gave him exercise.) When Ken tried to explain his preferences, they didn't seem to listen. And when he wanted to show off his latest baseball card or Christian CD, his mom and dad were not interested. Ken didn't know which bothered him more: their active disapproval or their passive disinterest.

Losing his CD player and "tunes" was pretty bad. But Ken was relieved that his dad had not also confiscated the baseball-card collection. Nor had Dad ordered him to get rid of them – only that he didn't want to see them again. Pulling another sturdy athletic shoebox from his closet, he began gathering his cards and angrily stacking them inside. He would keep his cards hidden when Dad was at home and pull them out only when Dad was away. It made him feel like a hunted spy in his own home. And the fact that his father had ripped off his music made him feel like a prisoner.

Just before 10:00 P.M., Ken climbed into bed for the night. He had not finished his homework. Tonight's clash with his dad had sapped him of the little motivation he'd had. He knew another incomplete assignment would pull down his grades even further. But what difference did it make? For all his trying, he couldn't seem to win with them. So why try?

Dad and Mom were in the family room watching TV as usual, so Ken knew they would not notice that his light was out. They seldom talked to him at bedtime anymore. No way did Ken want to return to his younger years when Dad or Mom tucked him in each night, read stories, said prayers and smothered him with kisses. That was okay for his younger sister, Hillary, but way too much for him. Yet no contact at bedtime didn't feel right either. It seemed that the only time his parents spoke to him was to criticize him or to correct him, and the only time they touched him was to push his feet off the sofa.

Lying in the darkness, Ken lifted a silent prayer. *God, I know You love me, but I'm not so sure Dad and Mom do. Why do they seem to be against everything I do? Why don't they care about my life, my feelings, my ideas and my interests? I know some things I do really tick them off. But they seem to disapprove of everything. It's like they're tired of being my parents. Why can't I get along with them, God?*

As he prayed, it occurred to Ken that home wasn't the only place where his relationships were wearing thin. The face of Todd Wallace, his friend at church, suddenly popped into his mind. Yeah, some friend,

Ken thought cynically. Todd is great to be around when we're doing what he wants to do. But when I ask him to go to the sports-card shop with me or if I need his help on a youth group outreach event, he is suddenly "too busy." It's like he's my friend when I fit in with his plans or when he needs something. Otherwise he could not care less.

Ken quickly added a postscript to his prayer. And, God, why can't Todd and I be real friends?

Just before drifting off to sleep, Ken thought about Doug Shaw. Doug and his wife, Jenny, were volunteer youth leaders at the church his family attended. A couple of years earlier, Doug had really helped Ken make the transition from getting by on his parents' faith to trusting Christ personally. Ken loved the youth group at church, and he considered Doug his spiritual big brother. Doug Shaw frequently told kids in the group that he and Jenny were available to talk with them about anything. For the first time since he had met Doug, Ken realized he had something he really wanted to talk about.

After school the next day, Ken walked to the small, downtown quick-print shop Doug and Jenny owned and operated. The shop was not exactly on Ken's way home, but he walked the extra six blocks anyway, hoping Doug was there and would have a minute to talk.

Walking into the shop, Ken felt a little odd. He had never done this before. Should he have made an appointment? What was he supposed to say? "Hey Doug, I have a problem. Will you stop working and solve it for me?" didn't sound too good. As it turned out, Ken didn't have to worry about it. Doug, who was doing a layout on one of the shop's computers, saw him come in the door.

"Hi, Ken," he said cheerfully, "what a nice surprise to have you drop in."

Jenny, who was waiting on a customer at the counter, also waved and smiled. Ken waved back. "Give me a couple of minutes, Ken," Doug called over the counter, "and I'll take a break. There's something I want to tell you. We can get something to drink."

"Sure," Ken said, nodding. Doug made him feel like a welcomed guest instead of an interruption in his schedule. It was a feeling he had been missing at home, where he sometimes felt like an intruder or a pest.

Five minutes later, Doug and Ken left the shop in Jenny's care and headed down the sidewalk toward a health-food shop called The Blender. As they walked, Doug grabbed Ken's shoulder and gave it a gentle squeeze. "I want to thank you for helping out with the sound during our youth outreach event last weekend," Doug said. "I saw you toting mike cords and speakers all over the place, and I appreciate your help."

Ken enjoyed getting caught doing something good for a change. He had worked hard with the sound crew during the big event, and he didn't think anybody had noticed.

"I enjoyed it," he said. "I'd like to work with sound again sometime."

They each bought a cold fruit smoothie then sat down together in a booth. They talked about the great music and dynamic speaker at the youth outreach event and the number of students who had trusted Christ as their Savior that night. Ken knew Doug had to get back to the shop soon. It would have been easy to skip the real reason he had come to see Doug. But he was afraid things would get much worse at home if he didn't talk to someone soon.

"I have kind of a prayer request to talk to you about, if you don't mind," Ken said, fiddling with the straw in his drink.

"I don't mind at all, Ken," Doug assured him.

"What can I pray with you about?"

Ken had told no one but God what he was about to reveal to Doug. The thought of actually telling another person about the anger and hurt he felt toward his parents and his friend Todd made him pause to swallow a surprising lump of emotion that had suddenly crept into his throat. "I'm ... I'm having trouble with my parents. We're not getting along very well right now." He briefly described the latest clash with his dad over the baseball cards. "It seems that everything I do is stupid or wrong. They're always ragging on me about my clothes or my music or my grades. They don't seem to care about who I am and what I like."

"Sometimes I feel like I'm living in the house alone. I don't know if they really love me." When he finished his explanation, Ken had tears in his eyes.

Doug's face clouded with sorrow. "Ken, I can see that this really hurts you. I'm sorry you are experiencing doubt about your parents' love. Seeing you in pain makes my heart hurt for you."

Ken felt some of the weight lift from him. Just knowing that Doug understood where he was coming from and hurt for him was a measure of relief he had not expected. Feeling his confidence swell, Ken went on to tell Doug about his recent difficulties in getting along with Todd Wallace.

After a few respectful moments, Doug said, "Tell me more about your relationship with your parents."

"What do you want to know?"

"How would you describe your relationship with your dad?"

Ken pulled the straw out of his drink and watched the juice drip into the glass. "If we're not talking about me – like what's wrong with what I'm doing and stuff – we usually don't talk. He's busy with his work and his hobbies."

"Does your dad ever have time for you?"

Ken shook his head slowly. "No."

"Do you feel like nothing you do is good enough for him?"

"Nothing I do is ever good enough for him," Ken emphasized, rubbing the hint of a small tear from his eye.

Doug asked several more questions about Ken's relationship with his parents. Then he gently probed into Ken's friendship with Todd. Each sad answer was accompanied by a shadow of sorrow on his face.

Finally Doug said, "I have to get back to the shop. But maybe we can get together again soon so we can talk more about the conflicts in your relationships and pray together. Would that be okay?"

"Yeah, that would be okay."

Since they both attended the 9:30 a.m. worship service on Sundays, they decided to meet at church during the 11:00 service. Doug said he knew about an empty Sunday-school classroom they could use then. Ken eagerly agreed.

"Until then," Doug said, "I want you to know that I care about you, Ken. I know it hurts to feel that your parents don't understand you and that Todd is so self-centered in his friendship toward you. I want to stay with you through this. I'll be praying for you. In fact, let me say a prayer for you right now."

Ken fought back another tear as Doug quietly asked God to share His comfort with Ken. When Doug said good-bye and returned to the shop, Ken was not eager to go home. He knew he would probably be quizzed and criticized for getting home late, and he sure couldn't tell Todd about his talk with Doug. But he felt a spark of comfort and encouragement knowing that he was not alone in his pain. Doug knew and cared, and that meant a lot to Ken. It gave him a glimmer of hope that someday his relationships with three important people in his life might get better.

# TIME OUT TO CONSIDER

IS YOUR RELATIONSHIP WITH YOUR PARENTS anything like Ken's? Do you seem to be at odds with them about practically everything? Do you hear more criticisms at home than compliments? Do your parents give you grief about your appearance, your manners (or lack of them), your room, your music, your friends, your grades, or your activities? Do they easily catch you doing things wrong and hardly ever notice when you do things right? Do many of your conversations end up as arguments or shouting matches? Does it seem that they are more interested in your brothers or sisters than in you? Do you sometimes wonder if your parents really love you?

In some families, parent/child conflicts may be so severe that they can be described as abusive. Some parents neglect their children's basic needs for shelter, food, clothing, medical attention, education and so on. Arguments deteriorate into physical attacks or vicious name-calling. Children in these kinds of homes should report physical, sexual, or emotional abuse to the proper authorities because of imminent danger to their life and health.

Yet in many homes, like Ken's, parents are not criminally negligent or abusive. In fact, Ken's Christian parents provide well for his basic needs, and they do not abuse him or his sister physically or sexually. However, they may be guilty of being inattentive to many of Ken's less obvious emotional needs.

This may be the case in your family. Your parents may provide a safe, healthy environment in which to live and care for your physical well-being. But you may struggle to get along because they don't seem to understand that you need more than three meals a day and a roof over your head to feel loved and accepted.

How about the other important relationships in your life? Are any of them like Ken's "friendship" with Todd? Are you on great terms with somebody one week and then strangers or enemies the next? Whether you are clashing with your parents, friends, or other people, the issue is the same. You have valid emotional needs, and when those needs are ignored, conflicts arise.

If this describes some of your relationships, it is important that you understand three things. First, it will be helpful for you to know why people are inattentive to some of your needs. Second, you must identify the specific needs in your life that are being overlooked or ignored by others. Third, it is important to understand how to talk to your parents and others about your needs. This booklet will help you in all three areas.

First, let's talk about why your parents may be unaware of your needs.

Parenting is a tough job, and there are no perfect parents. Adults must juggle many demands of life in addition to raising their children. With the pressures and responsibilities of marriage, career, finances and outside activities, many parents find it difficult to give their full attention and care to their children. There are a variety of reasons that parents may be inattentive to the needs of their children. Perhaps your parents are struggling with one or more of the following.

*Financial pressure*

Many parents work so hard each week to put food on the table and to pay the bills that their children are sometimes neglected. Some single parents must work two jobs to make ends meet, leaving little time for the children. In many two-parent homes, both Dad and Mom work full-time.

Financial pressures can be so exhausting that parents have little attention or energy left for their children.

*Hectic lifestyle*

Parents are often so involved with the demands of a busy life that some important things get left undone. Career, church and community activities may keep them going day and night. And the activities of their children – sports, school functions, music lessons, camps, church activities and more – just add to their hectic schedules.

Parents may be so busy doing things for and with their children that they overlook the important role of being attentive parents.

*Family breakup*

Divorce and single parenting create great stress on parents. One parent may be left with the parenting work of two. Extra financial burdens, the beginning of a new career or education track, and new relationships may distract the parent and make careful attention to each child seem impossible.

*Large families*

The more children there are in the family, the harder it may be to give appropriate attention and care to each.

*Self-centeredness*

Parents tend to neglect their children if they are constantly preoccupied with their own interests and activities. Their drive to climb the social ladder or to achieve status and wealth is sometimes elevated above the emotional needs of the children.

*Lack of parenting skills*

Some parents do not know how to meet all the needs of their children. Some believe that parenting only means providing for physical and material needs.

It is highly unlikely that your parents are purposely inattentive to your needs or disagreeable toward you and your lifestyle. Are one or more of the reasons above keeping them from meeting your needs?

Similar characteristics could be at the root of your conflicts. Mainly, your friends are sometimes clueless about your emotional needs because they are too busy with their own lives, because they are too self-centered, or because they lack the sensitivity and skills for being a caring, supportive friend.

Ken's concern over his relational conflicts has negatively affected his grades. His motivation and concentration have been dulled by a lack of encouragement and interest from his parents. How have your difficulties at home impacted your daily life? There are many negative effects that result when people don't get along. Perhaps you will identify with one or more of the following:

• You may feel worthless or unimportant.

• Your concentration and motivation in school may be weak, and your grades may suffer as a result.

• Lacking full acceptance from those you care about, you may be tempted to hang out with others who are a bad influence on your moral and spiritual values.

• You may have difficulty finding and developing

other good relationships.

• You may be tempted to rebel against your parents or to hurt your friend in order to gain their attention or to punish them for their lack of attentiveness.

• Lack of close interaction or caring in relationships may tempt you to get involved with alcohol or drugs.

• You may be tempted to find the intimacy you miss in sexual activity.


How are you dealing with your struggle to get along with others and the negative effects of this conflict in your life? Ken Meyers is a good example of how to respond. He went to a trusted Christian friend and mentor, Doug Shaw, and told him about his problems. You may experience a wide range of feelings about your conflicts. You may feel sad, depressed, hopeless, abandoned, frightened, and even angry. You may cry about what is happening. You may feel emotionally drained. Or you may get angry at the situation, at your parents or friends, or even at God for allowing it to happen.

It is important to understand that all these feelings are normal and natural. It is the way God wired you. Your emotions are a built-in release valve to help you handle the inner pain. Of course, there are both productive and unproductive ways of expressing these emotions.

When Ken went to Doug and poured out his story and hurt, he was taking the first healthy step in dealing with his situation. This response reflects Jesus' words in Matthew 5:4: "Blessed are those who mourn, for they will be comforted." Mourning is the process of getting the hurt out. You share how you feel so others can hurt with you. This is God's design for blessing you and for beginning to heal the pain that accompanies a difficult struggle in your relationships. It is good and necessary that you experience the different emotions that come at this time.

Your greatest need as you express your pain is for others to comfort you. That's what Doug was doing as Ken told his story, feeling Ken's pain and sharing the sorrow with him. In a time of emotional hurt, our greatest comfort comes when others sorrow with us. One major way God shares His comfort with us is through other people. The apostle Paul wrote, "God . . . comforts us in all our troubles, so that we can comfort those in any trouble with the comfort we ourselves have received from God" (2 Cor. 1:3,4).

What is comfort? Maybe it will help to see first

what comfort is not. Comfort is not a "pep talk" urging you to hang in there, to tough it out, or to hold it together. Comfort is not an attempt to explain why bad things happen to people. Comfort is not a bunch of positive words about God being in control and everything being okay. All of these things may be good and useful in time, but they do not fill our primary need for comfort.

People comfort us primarily by feeling our hurt and sorrowing with us. Jesus illustrated the ministry of comfort when His friend Lazarus died (see John 11). When Jesus arrived at the home of Lazarus's sisters, Mary and Martha, He wept with them (see vv. 33-35). His response is especially interesting in light of what He did next: raise Lazarus from the dead (see vv. 38-44).

Why didn't Jesus simply tell the grieving Mary and Martha, "No need to cry, My friends, because in a few minutes Lazarus will be alive again"? Because at that moment they needed someone to identify with their hurt. Jesus met Mary and Martha's need for comfort by sharing in their sorrow and tears. Later He performed the miracle that turned their sorrow to joy.

We receive comfort when we know we are not suffering alone. Paul instructed us, "Rejoice with those who rejoice; mourn with those who mourn"

(Rom. 12:15). When you experience sorrow, people may try to comfort you by cheering you up, urging you to be strong, or trying to explain away the tragic event. These people no doubt care about you and mean well by their words. But they may not know what comfort sounds like. Hopefully, there is also someone around like Doug Shaw who will provide the comfort you need. You will sense God's care and concern for you as this someone hurts with you, sorrows with you, and even weeps with you. Doug Shaw is a good example of what real comfort looks like in painful circumstances.

So your first response to your struggle is to share your burden with someone who cares about you. It may be a youth leader like Doug Shaw, your minister, or a mature, trusted Christian friend. But there is more to dealing with your situation than pouring out your story and receiving comfort, as Ken Meyers is about to find out.

# KEN'S STORY

**K**EN'S MIND WOULD OFTEN WANDER during sermons, but it was especially difficult to pay attention today. Sitting with his parents and his sister, Hillary, in the sanctuary, Ken considered the irony. To others in the church, the Meyerses probably looked like the ideal Christian family. But to Ken, this didn't feel like a family at all. His parents seemed more like jailers, restricting his privileges and general enjoyment of life until he had served his "sentence" and earned his freedom at age eighteen. Ken wondered if anything Doug Shaw could say would make a difference in his relationship with his dad and mom. He had similar doubts about his former good friend, Todd.

A little after 11:00 a.m. Ken met Doug in an empty Sunday school-classroom. Ken had not told his parents why he was meeting with Doug, only that Doug wanted to talk to him. Dad and Mom eagerly gave permission for Ken to stay, saying they would pick him up in front of the church at noon. They probably hope Doug will talk some sense into me about my "worldly" behavior, he thought cynically.

"How's it been going at home since we talked last week, Ken?" Doug began.

Ken shrugged. "About the same, I guess. It's like I'm not even part of the family. I live there and sleep there, but Dad and Mom don't notice me unless I do something they don't approve of – and they seem to find plenty of those things each week."

"I'm sad that you don't feel as close to your parents as you want to," Doug said. "I've been praying for you since we talked at The Blender because I really care about you."

Ken dropped his head sheepishly. "Thanks." Doug's prayers and concern meant more to him than he could express. "And thanks for the note you sent to me. It really helped."

"Let me ask you a question, Ken," Doug continued. "It will help us get into your struggles with your parents. And it will lead us to some guidelines that should help you at home and with your friend Todd."

Ken nodded. "Okay, shoot."

"Have you ever said something like 'Hey, Mom and Dad, I'm getting hungry. What's for dinner?'"

Ken raised an eyebrow, wondering where Doug was going with his question. "Of course, about five times a week. What do you mean by-"

Doug cut him off with his next question. "And do your parents always provide dinner and other meals for you?"

"Yeah, of course," Ken said, still wondering what food had to do with his problem. "And if they aren't around at mealtime, there is always something in the fridge I can nuke. Why do you ask?"

"Let me ask one more question, then I think you will understand," Doug said. "Have you ever said to your mom or dad, 'I'm really feeling ignored. Do you have fifteen minutes you can spend with me?'"

Ken studied Doug's expression, which conveyed that he had a secret he was just bursting to tell. "No way," Ken answered finally. "I mean, can you imagine any kid like me saying that to his parents? It never happens."

Doug pressed on. "But when you're hungry, you're not afraid to ask them for something to eat, right?"

"Right."

"Then why can't you express your other needs and respectfully ask your parents to meet them?"

Ken didn't answer because he didn't know what to say. He had never considered telling his parents what he really felt.

Apparently Doug wasn't expecting an answer because he kept talking. "From what you have told me, Ken, your relationship with your parents would probably improve if they just sat down and listened to you occasionally and showed a little interest in some of your activities."

Ken smiled at the incredible thought. "It sure couldn't hurt."

"And how would you feel if they started to notice your positive behavior and complimented you when you did something right?"

Ken gave a small laugh. "I'd feel like they were on drugs."

Doug grinned at the humor. Then he said, "Seriously, if your parents began treating you this way, would your relationship with them better meet your expectations? Would you sense that they love you?"

Ken didn't hesitate. "Of course, but-"

Doug interrupted him by holding up his hand like a stop sign. "How will your parents understand how you want to be treated unless you tell them?" He didn't wait for an answer. "You have emotional needs, Ken – everybody does. You tell your mom and dad about your physical hunger for food, and they fill that need. I believe if you tell them about your emotional hunger for attention and approval, they will try to meet those needs too, because I think they really do love you."

Ken felt a mild flash of panic. "What do you mean by 'tell them'?"

"I mean 'tell them,'" Doug explained with an impish smile. "Sit down with your parents, explain your needs, and respectfully ask for their help in meeting them. Try the same thing with Todd. You need to tell him what you feel you need out of your relationship."

Ken was on his feet and pacing. "I don't know if I can do that with my parents," he said nervously.

"Sure you can," Doug said, sounding rock-solid confident. "I'll even go with you if you want."

Ken stopped pacing. "You'll talk to my parents for me?"

"I'll talk to your parents with you," Doug corrected, "after you and I have talked and prayed together about your specific needs and how they are not being met."

Ken could hardly believe it. "You would really do that?"

"Only if you want me to," Doug said. "And once we have gone through the process with your parents, you will know how to talk to Todd."

"That would be great," Ken said, dropping back into his chair with a relieved sigh.

During the next forty minutes, Doug helped Ken think through and list on paper specific areas in which his relationship with his parents was strained. The discussion helped them to identify three of Ken's emotional needs that were not being met at home. Then they prayed together that God would prepare the way for a positive, productive meeting with Ken's parents. Finally, Doug suggested that they repeat the process after Ken cleared the air with his mom and dad.

When Ken's dad arrived to pick him up, Doug asked if he could stop by later in the afternoon for a visit. "Ken and I have something we want to share with you," he said cordially.

Mr. Meyers agreed.

Ken rode home in silence, already nervous about the meeting but also hopeful that something good was about to happen between him and his mom and dad.

# TIME OUT TO CONSIDER

**K**EN NEEDED A BIT MORE THAN THE comfort of his youth leader to get through the conflict with his parents and friend, and so do you. There are two more important elements that hopefully are being supplied to you.

First, you need the support of others. What's the difference between comfort and support? People supply comfort when they share your sorrow emotionally. People supply support by helping you in practical, useful ways. You need the help of people who are committed to obeying Galatians 6:2: "Carry each other's burdens, and in this way you will fulfill the law of Christ."

Think about how Doug Shaw supported Ken. In addition to being a source of comfort, Doug helped Ken think through the practical steps of identifying unmet emotional needs and then committed to meet with Ken's parents. It is one thing to have someone there to share your pain and sorrow in a conflict. It is something else to have one or more persons step in and help you resolve the conflict.

You may be tempted to ignore or to refuse the support offered by others. You may feel that you can handle it yourself, or you may not want to bother other people with your problems. Resist that temptation. God put Galatians 6:2 in the Bible because He knows there are times we should rely on the support of others. This is such a time. Let other people help you, and be grateful for their help. It is one of the ways God is providing for you at this time.

What if you need practical help and nobody offers it? Ask for it. There is nothing wrong with telling a trusted friend, youth leader, or minister about your need and asking for help. In most cases, people are more than willing to help out; they just don't know what needs to be done. Feel free to help people support you at this time by letting them know what you need.

Second, you need the encouragement of others. You receive encouragement when someone does something thoughtful to lift your spirits. Ken was encouraged by Doug's commitment to pray for him. He was encouraged by the affirming words Doug shared in writing and in person. And he was encouraged by Doug's willingness to work through the practical aspects of his conflict at home. Encouraging deeds like these may not seem as practical as solving problems, but they are just as necessary.

Once again, if you do not receive the encouragement you need, ask for it. It's okay to tell someone who cares about you, "I need a hug" or "I just need you to be with me for a while."

As Ken discovered, there are practical steps you can take to resolve your difficulties with others. When you don't get along with people, you may think that they are just being difficult and unreasonable. This may be partly true, but there is often a deeper issue. As Doug pointed out to Ken, the conflict may exist because some of your needs are not being met. Everyone has needs. We have physical needs for food, rest, and safety. We have spiritual needs for forgiveness, fellowship with God, and freedom from guilt and shame. And we also have emotional needs, such as the need for love, security, and a sense of belonging.

You need not be ashamed or embarrassed about being needy. God created us with these needs and provided the means for getting these needs met. Philippians 4:19 reads, "My God will meet all your needs according to his glorious riches in Christ Jesus."

This verse reveals three clear facts:

(1) God knows you have needs.

(2) God wants to meet your needs.

(3) God can meet your needs according to His glorious riches in Christ.

God meets some of your needs directly through His relationship with you. He is ultimately the source of all fulfilled needs, and He wants to see all your needs met. But He has chosen to meet a large number of your needs through relationships with others. At this point in your life, your relationship with your parents is His primary avenue for meeting many of your emotional needs. He may use other family members, church leaders and friends to meet some of your needs, but your parents are the key instruments God uses for meeting your needs, including emotional needs.

What are your emotional needs? Like Ken, you may not know how to answer that question.

And it is possible that your parents and friends are not meeting some of your emotional needs because they have not identified them either. Just imagine what could happen in your relationships if you could identify some needs, share them with your parents, and begin to work with Dad and Mom – instead of against them – to see those needs met. Think how that same process could help clear up conflicts between you.

Six common emotional needs often go unmet in relationships. They are the need for attention, appreciation, approval, acceptance, respect, and affection. God created us with these needs, and He gave us parents and others to help meet them. Conflicts between people often arise when these needs are neither identified nor communicated. Like Doug said, you tell your parents when you feel hungry and in need of food. Why not tell them when you are needy emotionally so they can better meet those needs?

As you read about these six needs, two or three of them may stand out to you. They are likely your most pressing emotional needs at this time. At some point in the future, it will be helpful for you to talk to your parents about them.

## Attention

Our need for attention is met when someone shows interest and concern for who we are and what we do. If any of the following statements are true of you, perhaps your need for attention is not being fully met in your closest relationships:

• My parents or friends don't ever listen to me.

• My parents or friends don't have time for me.

• I often feel ignored by my parents or friends.

• Dad and Mom rarely do anything with me.

• My friends never want to do what I want to do.

• My parents almost never come to anything I'm involved in (concerts, ball games, etc).

## Appreciation

We feel appreciated when others share words of gratitude or praise for what we do. If you can identify with any of these statements, your need for appreciation is not being fully met:

• My parents seldom notice when I do something around the house.

• Mom and Dad talk about my bad behavior but hardly ever mention the good things.

• I don't think my parents or friends are aware of my positive qualities.

• I hardly ever hear the words "Thank you" from my parents or friends.

*Approval*

Our need for approval is met when others compliment our deeds and speak well of us. These statements reflect a student whose need for approval is not being met by parents or friends. Are they true of you?

• Nothing I do is good enough for my parents or friends.

• My parents or friends don't approve of me.

• It seems that my parents or friends criticize me all the time.

• My parents or friends sometimes make me feel like a complete failure.

# Conflict with Others

## Acceptance

We feel accepted when people know we are different and imperfect and love us anyway. Someone who doesn't feel accepted may make these statements:

• My parents or friends only seem to care about me if I do what they want me to do.

• Dad and Mom can't accept the fact that I'm different from them.

• Sometimes I feel like I don't belong in this family.

• They treat me like I don't know anything.

• When I mess up, my parents or friends can't seem to forgive me.

## Respect

Our need for respect is met when we feel highly valued and esteemed by others. You may identify with the following statements if you don't feel respected by your parents:

• My parents or friends are always yelling at me.

• I don't have any privacy at home.

• I feel like my parents or friends don't trust me.

• Mom and Dad treat me like a little kid.

• My parents are always checking up on me.

*Affection*

Affection is communicated through physical closeness and loving words. A lack of parent/child affection is reflected in the following statements:

• It seems that my parents treat my brother or sister better than they treat me.

• I wish I felt closer to my parents or friends.

• My parents hardly ever tell me they love me.

• Dad and Mom seldom hug or kiss me anymore.

• I don't receive much affection from my parents or friends.

• I know my parents love me, but sometimes they don't act like it.

Which are your two or three greatest unmet needs among these six? Prayerfully and respectfully share these needs with your parents and friends and see how you can work together to get your needs met.

At the same time, you must remember that meeting needs in relationships is a two-way street. Your parents and friends also have needs for attention, appreciation, approval, acceptance, respect and affection. You should not feel that you are the primary source for meeting these needs. But there may be ways you can help meet these needs, further improving your relationships.

How do you approach your parents or friends to share your needs with them? Ken Meyers is about to find out, with the help of his youth leader and friend, Doug Shaw.

# KEN'S STORY

**K**EN WAS SO NERVOUS THAT HIS VOICE squeaked when he spoke. He couldn't help it.

"Mom and Dad, I've been talking to Doug recently, and he has really helped me see some things in my life more clearly."

It was late Sunday afternoon, and he was seated with his parents in the family room of their home.

Doug Shaw was sitting nearby. Ken's younger sister, Hillary, was at a friend's house for the afternoon.

Ken went on. "As we talked, I came to better appreciate how well you take care of me. I mean, you provide a nice, safe home and plenty to eat. You buy most of my clothes and stuff for me. I just want you to know that I'm thankful for all you do. I know I don't tell you that enough." Ken swallowed hard. "And I ... I love you both."

He noticed a glimmer of a smile on their faces.

"We love you too, Kenneth," his Mom said. Dad nodded.

Ken cleared his throat. He found it very difficult to say these words, and he wished he could leave the room and let Doug do the talking for him. But he knew he had to go on.

"Since you are so good at taking care of my needs, we-er, I mean, /-want to tell you about a couple of other areas where I kind of need your help. Would that be okay?"

"Of course, Ken," Dad said, and both his parents waited expectantly.

Ken squirmed uncomfortably in his seat, glanced at Doug for encouragement, then began.

"Well, I'm learning that I have a pretty big need

for your approval. I know I screw up a lot, and you tell me about it when I do. I need to be corrected sometimes. But it would help me if you'd also mention when I do something right. I just need to hear that you approve of me in some areas. When I don't hear your approval, I begin to think everything I do is wrong. If either of you notices something I do right, would you be willing to tell me about it?"

Ken was too nervous to look his parents in the eye. He stole a glance at Doug, who flashed him a "good job" smile. Then he waited.

After several silent seconds, his Dad said, "Do you really think we don't approve of you?"

"Sometimes, Dad, when I only hear that my grades aren't good enough, that you don't like my clothes, that my room is messy ..." Ken could have added more to the list, but he didn't want to overdo it.

"Kenneth, you're our son," his Dad said, "and we're very proud of you. We only discipline you because we want the best for you."

Ken nodded. "I know, Dad. But when all I hear about is what needs to change, I get discouraged. It's like the other night, when you took away my CD player. I was working on my homework, and it was half done. But you didn't see that. Instead, all I heard about was how bad my music and study habits are."

Doug cut in respectfully. "Ken, maybe it would help if you told your Dad what you'd like to hear him say in a situation like the other night."

Ken thought for a moment. Then, turning toward his dad, he said, "I would have felt better if you said something like, 'How is your homework going?' And when I showed you my worksheet, you might say, 'Good job so far. If you need any help, ask me. Just don't let the music distract you.'"

Feeling more confident, Ken watched his Dad process his comment. After several moments, his father began to nod. "I think I see what you mean, son. I didn't realize I was so one-sided. I'm sorry I was hard on you the other night, and at other times too. I guess I am so eager for you to succeed that I forget to notice when you do succeed. I'm very sorry, Ken. Will you forgive me?"

Before Ken could respond, his Mother also apologized for not being more approving and asked his forgiveness. When Ken verbalized his forgiveness, Mom said, "We'll do our best to notice your strengths and good behavior and mention them to you."

Greatly encouraged by his parents' positive response, Ken went on to his second big need: for their attention. He explained the loneliness and frustration he felt when they didn't listen to him, spend time with him, or show an interest in his activities. "It would be great sometimes," he concluded, "if you could just come into my room, ask how I'm doing, and listen to me." His parents apologized again and promised to be more attentive.

Ken was prepared to stop there. He could hardly believe his parents' positive response to his words, and he didn't want to overburden them with his feelings. But Mom said, "This is very helpful to us, Kenneth. We didn't know how hurt you were feeling. Is there anything else?"

"Well, maybe one more thing," he said, glancing at Doug for another boost of courage. "When Doug and I talked, I realized I also have a big need for ... affection. I'm not a kid anymore, and I don't need to hold your hand everywhere we go. But I kind of miss the hugs, and I still like to hear you say 'I love you.'"

Ken's Mom was on her feet immediately with tears filling her eyes. "I'm so happy to hear you say that, Ken. I haven't hugged you as much lately because I thought you didn't want to be treated like a child. I have a lot more hugs and kisses for you."

Standing to meet her, Ken received his Mom's tearful embrace. In seconds Dad was there, too, and they all held each other until the three of them were crying. Then Doug Shaw joined in and prayed a short prayer for the Meyers family.

"There's just one thing," Ken said, wiping away tears with the back of his hand. There was a smile of mischief on his face. "I want hugs and kisses, but not when my friends are around, okay?" The four of them enjoyed a good, long laugh.

A few minutes later, when Doug explained that he had to leave, Ken walked him to the front door. "Thanks a lot Doug, for ... you know ... just, thanks."

"No problem, Ken," Doug returned. "I think it turned out well. You did a great job, and your parents ... well, I think they really love you."

Ken grinned and nodded. Doug opened the door and stepped out on the porch, then he turned to face his young friend. "Are you feeling okay about talking to Todd? Do you want me to go with you?"

Ken thought for a moment. "Thanks for offering, Doug, but I'll be okay. Talking to my folks today really helped me see how I need to talk to Todd. I think I can do it by myself . . . except for your prayers, of course."

"I know you can do it, Ken," Doug affirmed as he stepped off the porch, "and I will be praying for you.

Just let me know how it turns out." Then he waved and turned toward his car.

"Will do" Ken called after him. Closing the door, he was almost excited about clearing the air with his friend Todd. And he would enjoy talking to Doug – and his parents – about the meeting afterward.

# TIME OUT
# TO CONSIDER

**O**NCE YOU HAVE IDENTIFIED TWO OR three emotional needs that are not being fully met at home, plan a meeting with your parents to share those needs. This may sound difficult, especially if you are not comfortable being vulnerable with people. But it is necessary if you want your relationship with Dad and Mom to improve.

Here are several steps that will help you prepare.

# Conflict with Others

*Decide if you want someone else to go with you.*

Ken was grateful to have the counsel and encouragement of his youth leader. Perhaps you would feel more confident about meeting your parents if someone joined you. If you have shared your hurt with a youth leader or minister, that person may be willing to go along when you meet with your parents.

*Schedule a time to meet.*

Find a time and place for your meeting that will be free from interruptions and distractions. You might say to your parents, "I have something important I want to talk to you about. What would be a good time and place to sit down and talk for an hour?" Try to set up the meeting as soon as possible, while your unmet emotional needs are fresh in your mind.

*Prepare prayerfully.*

Ask God to give you a pure heart and good attitude for sharing. Ask Him to help you express your thoughts and concerns lovingly and in ways your parents will clearly understand and readily receive. Decide what you will say ahead of time. Try writing down your thoughts so you can read them to your parents.

*Express your love.*

Begin the meeting by verbalizing your love and gratitude for your parents. Focus on the positive aspects of your relationship. Thank them for what they do for you. Assure them that you are interested in seeing your relationship grow even stronger.

*Share your unmet emotional needs.*

Stay away from accusative "you" statements: "You make me so angry"; "You never spend any time with me"; or "You love my brother/sister more than me." Instead, use less threatening "I" statements: "I feel ignored and alone when we don't spend time together"; or "I like it when I hear compliments from you."

*Ask for – don't demand – their assistance.*

Say something like, "Dad and Mom, will you help me improve our relationship by trying to meet more of my need for respect?"

*Offer to make changes in your behavior.*

Ask your parents how you can help improve the relationship by your being more respectful, affectionate, or accepting. Tell them you are committed to changing your behavior to improve the relationship.

*Pray together.*

Consider asking your parents to pray with you for God's guidance and help as you seek to be more considerate of each other's needs.

In the weeks following Ken's meeting with his parents, their relationship began to improve. His parents became more considerate about commenting on Ken's good behavior, spent more time with him, and gave him more hugs. Ken worked at being more appreciative of his parents' love and provision for him. Whenever Dad or Mom displayed approval, attention, or affection, he thanked them for it.

Encouraged by his parents' response, Ken prepared to talk to his friend Todd in much the same way as he had prepared to talk to his parents. He realized that Todd was not meeting his need for respect as a friend, and he prayed that God would help him convey this concern to Todd. When they met, Todd was not as eager to deal with their differences as Ken's parents had been. But Ken felt good about their talk and determined to keep praying that his friendship with Todd would grow stronger.

Ken's relationship with his parents is not perfect. They still experience misunderstandings and disagreements from time to time. But things are getting much better since Ken respectfully sought his parents' help in meeting his needs. And Ken has the same hopes for his friendship with Todd.

There is hope for your relationships too. It all begins with identifying your hurts and needs, sharing them with your parents or friend, and helping each other make the relationship better.

## ABOUT THE AUTHORS

JOSH MCDOWELL is an internationally known speaker, author and traveling representative of Campus Crusade for Christ, International. He has authored or co-authored more than fifty books, including *Right from Wrong* and *Josh McDowell's Handbook on Counseling Youth*. Josh and his wife, Dottie, have four children and live in Dallas, Texas.

ED STEWART is the author or co-author of numerous Christian books. A veteran writer, Ed Stewart began writing fiction for youth as a co-author with Josh McDowell. He has since authored four suspense novels for adults. Ed and his wife, Carol, live in Hillsboro, Oregon. They have two grown children and four grandchildren.

**CHRISTIAN FOCUS PUBLICATIONS**

Christian Focus | Christian Heritage | CF4K | Mentor

Christian Focus Publications publishes books for adults and children under its four main imprints: Christian Focus, CF4K, Mentor and Christian Heritage. Our books reflect that God's word is reliable and Jesus is the way to know him, and live for ever with him.

Our children's publication list includes a Sunday School curriculum that covers pre-school to early teens; puzzle and activity books. We also publish personal and family devotional titles, biographies and inspirational stories that children will love.

If you are looking for quality Bible teaching for children then we have an excellent range of Bible story and age specific theological books.

From pre-school to teenage fiction, we have it covered!

## Find us at our web page:
## www.christianfocus.com